THE POWER OF
CURIOSITY

Emily A. Jordan

Contents

INTRODUCTION

Picture a world without computers. No smartphones, no laptops, and no video games. Hard to imagine, isn't it? Yet back in the early 1800s, the idea of a machine that could calculate numbers or follow instructions seemed like science fiction—until a brilliant mathematician named Ada Lovelace had a groundbreaking vision.

Ada was born into a world of fancy dresses, horse-drawn carriages, and candlelit libraries. She was part of Britain's high society, known for grand balls and strict rules about what women could and couldn't do. But Ada dared to break those rules by diving headfirst into mathematics and mechanics. At a time when most women didn't receive serious schooling, she pored over geometry, studied how machines worked, and collaborated with some of the greatest scientific minds of her day.

One of those minds was Charles Babbage, an inventor with a wild plan to build mechanical "engines" that could perform complex calculations. Most people scratched their heads, but Ada saw something that no one else did: these machines might do more than just math. She believed they could be programmed to handle any kind of information—words, music, even pictures—if they were given the right instructions. This idea was the spark that eventually led to modern computing.

Yet Ada's life wasn't all smooth sailing. She battled health issues and had to balance her mathematical dreams with family responsibilities. Some people dismissed her ideas as impossible. But Ada refused to let doubts stop her. Through her grit and genius, she laid the foundations for the computer algorithms that shape our digital world today—more than a century before any actual computer was built!

Get ready to step into Victorian England and discover how a curious, determined young woman became the very first computer programmer in history. You'll learn about mechanical engines that used punch cards, find out why math was Ada's favorite subject, and see how her story still inspires the innovators of tomorrow. Turn the page to meet Ada Lovelace, the visionary who dreamed of computers long before the world was ready.

Chapter 1: A Most Unusual Childhood

Ada Lovelace was born on December 10, 1815, to parents who couldn't have been more different. Her father was Lord George Gordon Byron, a famous poet who was both celebrated and controversial in England. Her mother was Lady Annabella Milbanke Byron, a highly educated woman who loved math and was nicknamed the "Princess of Parallelograms." Despite these intriguing nicknames, Lord Byron and Lady Byron didn't get along at all.

Just weeks after Ada's birth, her parents separated. Lord Byron left England and never returned, so Ada never really knew her father, though she heard plenty of stories about him. Her mother, determined that Ada would not inherit her father's "wild imagination" (as she saw it), decided to emphasize logic, order, and mathematics in Ada's upbringing. From a young age, Ada was surrounded by tutors, governesses, and books filled with numbers and geometric shapes.

In the early 1800s, it was rare for a girl—especially one from the upper class—to study math and science so seriously. Society expected young ladies to learn music, drawing, manners, and perhaps a bit of French. But Lady Byron insisted that Ada take lessons in arithmetic, geometry, and even astronomy. She hoped that rigorous thinking would keep Ada's mind steady, rather than drifting into poetry and drama like her father.

Ada's childhood wasn't just about memorizing formulas, though. She had a vivid imagination, often drawing pictures of new inventions she dreamed up. At times, she was confined to bed due to poor health—she suffered from migraines and other ailments that left her weak for weeks at a time. But even when stuck in bed, she read eagerly about science and machines, covering her notebooks with sketches of flying contraptions. She once tried to design a mechanical bird that could actually fly, studying the wings of real birds to figure out wing spans and angles.

This mix of creativity and logic set Ada apart. She was a mathematician at heart, yet she never forgot the importance of imagination in solving problems. While her mother encouraged her analytical side, Ada quietly let her mind roam in curious ways—often thinking, "What if?" For instance, "What if machines could do more than just simple tasks? What if they could understand patterns, or even play music, if we 'taught' them how?"

By the time Ada was a teenager, she'd earned a reputation among her tutors as an unusually bright student with a passion for numbers. She devoured math textbooks and corresponded with professors who were amazed by her enthusiasm. Yet Ada's life was also constrained by the expectations of high society—hosting parties, wearing fancy gowns, and making polite conversation. Whenever she could, she escaped back into her studies, where she felt most alive.

Little did Ada know, her path was about to cross with one of Britain's most inventive minds, a man named Charles Babbage, who was working on a machine he called the Difference Engine. Their meeting would ignite a collaboration that would change how people thought about machines forever. But for now, Ada was a curious girl, juggling the pressures of Victorian life with her burning desire to explore the mysterious world of mathematics.

Chapter 2: Meeting Charles Babbage

The year was 1833, and Ada was just 17 when she attended a party where Charles Babbage was showing off a small part of his invention, the Difference Engine. Imagine a room lit by flickering candles, filled with elegantly dressed guests sipping tea and making polite conversation. Amid the clinking of teacups, Ada's eyes were drawn to a curious mechanical device: a maze of gears, levers, and metal parts. This was Babbage's Difference Engine prototype, designed to perform mathematical calculations automatically.

At the time, calculations for navigation, astronomy, or engineering projects were done by hand. One mistake in arithmetic could throw off entire projects. Babbage's idea was to eliminate human error by building a machine that used clockwork precision to add and subtract. It was a revolutionary concept—though the project was plagued by funding problems and technical difficulties.

Yet when Ada saw the machine, she didn't just see a fancy calculator. She saw potential. She was fascinated by how the gears turned, how the machine "remembered" numbers, and how it could produce accurate results. So much so that she peppered Babbage with questions: "Could it do more complex operations?" "How would the results be printed?" Ada's intelligence and enthusiasm immediately caught Babbage's attention. Here was a young woman who understood his invention's promise on a deeper level than most adults in the room.

Impressed by Ada, Babbage agreed to become something of a mentor. Though more than 20 years older, he recognized in her a kindred spirit—someone who believed in the power of mechanical computation. Babbage was already dreaming of a more advanced machine he called the Analytical Engine, which would be programmable to handle not just one type of calculation but many. While others struggled to grasp why anyone would need such a machine, Ada was captivated.

Over the next few years, Ada and Babbage exchanged letters about mathematics, logic, and machinery. Babbage saw her not just as a student but as a collaborator. He invited her to see prototypes, shared his notes, and asked for her thoughts on how certain parts of the Engine might work. Ada was thrilled. The more she learned, the more she believed that machines could be programmed to follow sequences of instructions—like "If you see this number, do this operation next."

Meanwhile, society whispered about Ada's curious friendship with an older inventor. Women of her status typically socialized at balls or wrote letters about fashion, not advanced mathematics. But Ada wasn't about to let gossip keep her away from the most exciting intellectual pursuit of her life.

As Babbage's ideas for the Analytical Engine grew, so did Ada's. She began to think beyond basic arithmetic, wondering if these "engines" could handle tasks in symbolic form. After all, she reasoned, music and letters could also be converted into numbers. If you could translate notes into code and feed them into a machine, might it produce music? This was a giant leap in thinking—no one else was considering such possibilities in the early 1800s.

Still, Babbage's invention was far from finished. He struggled to secure government funding, and building the machine from metal parts required extreme precision. At every turn, Babbage battled bureaucrats, soared over budget, and faced skepticism from those who called his ideas fantasy. Yet he kept refining his plans, buoyed by Ada's unwavering belief that the Analytical Engine could transform mathematics and more.

Ada continued her own studies, working with notable mathematicians like Augustus De Morgan. De Morgan taught her advanced calculus, further sharpening her ability to think abstractly. This education would soon prove critical when she took on the project that would make her famous in the history of computing.

Neither Ada nor Babbage knew it yet, but a moment was coming that would require Ada to put her mathematical gifts to the test. When that chance arrived, she would write a set of notes so forward-thinking, so radical, that they would shape how future generations understood the power of computers—and earn Ada Lovelace the title of the world's first computer programmer.

CHAPTER 3: THE ANALYTICAL ENGINE AND ADA'S NOTES

In 1842, an Italian engineer named Luigi Menabrea wrote a paper describing Charles Babbage's Analytical Engine in French. Babbage asked Ada Lovelace to translate Menabrea's paper into English, thinking she was the perfect person for the job, given her bilingual skills and deep knowledge of the machine. But translating turned out to be only half of what Ada did.

While working on the translation, Ada added a series of notes labeled A through G, which ended up being much longer than Menabrea's original paper. These notes were packed with Ada's own insights about the Analytical Engine's potential. She explained how the machine could handle not just numbers but any data that could be represented by numbers—letters, symbols, even musical notes.

Within these notes lay her most groundbreaking contribution: an example of how the Analytical Engine could be given a sequence of steps to compute Bernoulli numbers, a concept from advanced mathematics. In modern terms, we'd call this a computer program—a set of instructions telling a machine exactly what to do step by step. No one had ever written such detailed instructions for a general-purpose computing device before.

Ada also used her notes to discuss an idea that wouldn't become mainstream for another century: the possibility of artificial intelligence. She theorized that while the Engine could follow instructions, it couldn't originate new ideas on its own. It needed a human to program it. This speculation about whether machines could "think" in the future put Ada far ahead of her time.

For Babbage, Ada's notes were an exhilarating glimpse into what his Engine might achieve someday. For Ada, writing the notes was a marathon of mental effort. She spent months pouring over calculations, rewriting sections, and double-checking each line of her Bernoulli number program. Her health problems flared up again— she often worked while lying down, writing letters and scribbling equations in bed. Yet she was driven by a fierce conviction that she was doing something important.

Finally, in 1843, the paper, along with Ada's notes, was published in an English journal. Instead of just being a translation of Menabrea's work, it became a comprehensive vision of what the Analytical Engine could do. Readers who dared to wade through the dense math were stunned. While Babbage was known for his mechanical brilliance, Ada's notes added a new level of theoretical understanding—the notion that machines could process any type of information if it could be broken down into symbols.

Some people mocked the idea as "far-fetched." After all, Babbage's Engine existed mostly on paper, with only small prototypes constructed. Others praised Ada's intellect, calling her a genius. But the society she lived in didn't quite know how to handle a woman who wrote advanced math papers. Ada shrugged off the doubters, pushing ahead with more plans, more calculations. She even dreamed of applying her methods to music composition, though she never had the chance to fully explore that idea.

The historical significance of those notes wouldn't be fully appreciated until the 20th century, when real computers began to appear. Early computer pioneers like Alan Turing and others recognized that Ada had described many of the fundamental principles behind programming long before anyone else. Today, Ada's notes are considered a milestone in the history of computing, and she's often hailed as the world's first computer programmer.

But for Ada, the journey wasn't over. She still had challenges ahead, both personal and scientific, and her continued attempts to work with Babbage on the Analytical Engine would run into obstacles—funding, health issues, and Babbage's own unyielding perfectionism. Yet in the midst of those struggles, Ada's unwavering faith in technology's future never wavered. She had looked at a machine of gears and rods and seen the seeds of a digital tomorrow.

CHAPTER 4: VISION BEYOND NUMBERS

One of the most remarkable things about Ada Lovelace's work is how she viewed the Analytical Engine as something far greater than a giant calculator. In her famous notes, she wrote that the Engine "might act upon other things besides number." This was a radical claim in an era when even the idea of a mechanical device doing math automatically was hard for most people to grasp.

For Ada, numbers were symbols, and if music, words, or images could be converted into those symbols, then a machine following precise instructions could manipulate them. This wasn't just an upgrade to arithmetic—it was the seed of what we now call general-purpose computing. Today, we take for granted that our devices can handle text, images, sound, and video. But in the mid-19th century, no one else was discussing that possibility, at least not in such a detailed, mathematical way.

Ada also wrestled with philosophical questions about artificial intelligence. She wrote that "the Analytical Engine has no pretensions whatever to originate anything. It can do whatever we know how to order it to perform." In other words, machines could follow rules set by humans but didn't have creativity of their own—at least in her view. It was a nuanced stance, showing she'd considered the Machine's potential to learn or create autonomously, but concluded that it was limited by the instructions given by humans.

This standpoint—often called the "Lovelace objection" in modern AI discussions—still sparks debate among computer scientists. Can machines truly invent new ideas, or are they confined to whatever algorithms humans provide? Ada's early thoughts on the subject laid the groundwork for these debates, showing once again how far ahead of her time she really was.

Her vision also extended to practical applications. Ada believed that machines like the Analytical Engine could help scientists handle long, tedious calculations more reliably, freeing them to do more creative work. She saw a future where a single machine might be used for different tasks simply by changing its instructions, a concept we now associate with computer "programming." This was a dramatic departure from specialized machines that could only do one job.

Yet Ada didn't stop at theory. She wrote her elaborate example program for calculating Bernoulli numbers, showing exactly how the machine's gears and wheels could be "told" to carry out each step. It was a model for how we still write software—breaking down a task into smaller parts and specifying an order in which the machine should execute those parts.

This broad-minded view of computing as something beyond plain arithmetic is what cements Ada Lovelace's legacy as an innovator in computer science, even though she lived and died before any real computer existed. Her ideas about the versatility of machines foretold the age of digital electronics, where everything from music streaming to word processing relies on data processed by general-purpose devices.

Of course, Ada wasn't alone in pushing the boundaries—Charles Babbage paved the way with his mechanical designs, and many mathematicians contributed to the knowledge of logic and number theory that underpins computing. But Ada's unique blend of rigorous math training, imaginative spirit, and deep engagement with Babbage's concepts gave her a special vantage point. In the 21st century, her name resonates as an emblem of female achievement in STEM fields, showing that brilliance transcends all barriers—time, gender, or societal expectations.

CHAPTER 5: CHALLENGES, SETBACKS, AND PERSEVERANCE

Ada Lovelace may have had brilliant insights, but her life was far from easy. She faced obstacles both personal and societal, many of which threatened to derail her mathematical pursuits.

Societal Expectations

As the daughter of nobility in Victorian England, Ada was expected to marry well and devote herself to household affairs. Indeed, she married William King, who became the Earl of Lovelace, making Ada a countess. This title came with many social duties—hosting parties, visiting other nobles, and managing household staff. While Ada carried out these responsibilities, she often found them dull compared to the thrill of mathematics. She carved out time for her studies by rising early or staying up late, sacrificing leisure and rest to continue her work.

Health Struggles

Physical ailments plagued Ada from childhood. Migraines, digestive problems, and other illnesses frequently confined her to bed. Despite these setbacks, she used her downtime to read, calculate, and write letters—sometimes with the paper resting on a lap desk while she lay under blankets. Medicines and treatments in the 1800s were often rudimentary, and Ada endured treatments that sometimes worsened her symptoms. Yet she refused to let poor health silence her mind.

Babbage's Funding Woes

While Ada's brilliance shone in her Notes on the Analytical Engine, the actual machine remained mostly theoretical. Charles Babbage struggled to secure government funding for the project, and private investors were wary of pouring money into a device no one could fully comprehend. Without a working machine, Ada's programming ideas couldn't be tested in real life. Over time, even Ada grew frustrated with Babbage's inability to finish building the Engine, though she never stopped believing in its potential.

Misjudged Ventures

Later in life, Ada's ambitious mind led her to dabble in various pursuits, including schemes to apply mathematical methods to horse racing bets—a venture that ended badly. She hoped to use probability to forecast winners, but the plan went awry, leaving her in debt.

Some critics seized on this failure to mock her intelligence, but Ada saw it as a lesson in risk and the complexities of real-world data.

Family Tensions

Ada's relationship with her mother was always complicated. Lady Byron wanted Ada to be disciplined in mathematics, partly to avoid the "dangerous" creativity that marked Lord Byron's poetic life. While Ada appreciated her mother's support, she also felt pressure to suppress her imaginative side. In later years, they had disagreements about finances and Ada's social circle. Still, Lady Byron was one of the few people who recognized Ada's genius and tried to nurture it despite societal norms.

Despite all these challenges, Ada never abandoned her passion for math and innovation. In her letters, she spoke of an "insatiable thirst" for understanding the universe, whether through numbers or machines. This unwavering drive is what kept her going, fueling her creation of the first computer program and her visionary thoughts on the future of technology.

CHAPTER 6: LATER LIFE AND LEGACY

Ada Lovelace's later years were marked by continued intellectual curiosity and a desire to push the boundaries of what machines and mathematics could achieve. However, her health continued to decline, and family matters increasingly took up her time. She had three children with the Earl of Lovelace and tried to balance motherhood with her studies—no easy feat in any era, let alone Victorian England.

Collaborations and Correspondence

Even as she managed household duties, Ada kept up a lively correspondence with scientists, mathematicians, and philosophers. She exchanged letters with Michael

Faraday, the famous physicist who studied electromagnetism, and she kept track of new scientific discoveries by reading whatever she could get her hands on. Although she never completed another major scholarly work after her Notes, these connections kept her at the forefront of intellectual debate.

Increasing Health Woes

By her mid-30s, Ada's health took a severe turn for the worse. She was diagnosed with what many historians believe was uterine cancer, and the treatments of the time did little to ease her suffering. Despite the pain, she continued to express her hopes that one day Babbage's Analytical Engine might be completed, or that some other inventor would take up the mantle. She never lived to see a working computer, but she never lost faith in the power of a machine to handle complex tasks with the right instructions.

A Quiet Passing

Ada Lovelace died on November 27, 1852, at the age of 36—tragically young by modern standards. In her final days, she expressed regret that she hadn't done more, and she reconciled with her mother to some extent. She was buried next to her father, Lord Byron, though they had never truly known each other in life.

Rediscovery of Her Genius

For a long time after her death, Ada's contributions were overlooked. Charles Babbage's unfinished engines were more a curiosity than a recognized stepping stone to the modern computer. But in the early 20th century, researchers who studied the history of computing stumbled upon Ada's Notes. They realized that she had envisioned the principles of computing long before actual computers existed.

By the 1970s, Ada Lovelace was being celebrated as the first computer programmer. Her name began to appear in textbooks and scholarly papers, and tech communities recognized her as a pioneer. In 1979, the U.S. Department of Defense developed a computer language named "Ada" in her honor, reflecting her status as a foundational figure in software development.

Today, her memory is kept alive through conferences, awards, and educational initiatives encouraging women and girls to explore STEM fields (Science, Technology, Engineering, and Mathematics). She's viewed as an example of how determination, creativity, and a willingness to question the norms can lead to ideas that change the world—even if it takes decades for the world to catch up.

As you continue reading about Ada's life and work, remember that her story is one of triumph over adversity, vision against doubt, and genius that flourished despite every obstacle Victorian society could throw at her. If you've ever typed code into a computer or used an app on your phone, you've stepped into a realm Ada Lovelace helped create—proving that her legacy endures every time

we press "Enter."

Chapter 7: Fun Activity Section

Are you ready to think like Ada Lovelace? Here are two activities that bring her ideas about instructions and symbolic representation to life!

Activity 1: Create Your Own "Punch Card" Code

Materials

- Index cards (or cut-up cardstock)

- Hole punch

- Pencil

- A "code key" you create (explained below)

Instructions

1. Invent a Simple Code: Assign numbers or symbols to letters of the alphabet. For instance, A = 01, B = 02, and so on. Write these on a separate piece of paper as your "code key."

2. Punch Cards: For each letter or symbol you want to represent, punch holes in the index card in positions that match your code. For example, if "C" = 03, you might punch 3 holes in a specific row or column.

3. Decode: Have a friend try to "read" your punch card code using the key. See if they can decipher the message!

What You Learn

Ada Lovelace helped pioneer the idea that numbers could be instructions for a machine. Punch cards were later used in early computers to feed in "data." By making your own, you'll see how bits of information can be stored and read in a pattern of holes—just like symbolic representation!

Activity 2: Writing a Simple "Algorithm"

Materials

- Paper

- Pencil or marker

Instructions

1. Pick a Task: Choose a simple daily task (like making a sandwich or brushing your teeth).

2. Write Step-by-Step: Break it down into the smallest possible steps. For making a peanut butter

sandwich: "1) Open the jar. 2) Insert knife. 3) Scoop peanut butter. 4) Spread on bread...."

3. Test It: Hand your "algorithm" to a friend. Can they follow it exactly as written? If they get stuck, rewrite the instructions more precisely.

What You Learn

Ada's genius was recognizing that machines could follow a set of instructions—an algorithm—if those steps were clear and logical. Just like you're telling your friend how to make a sandwich, programmers tell a computer how to solve a problem, one line of code at a time!

CHAPTER 8: TIMELINE

Follow the key events in Ada Lovelace's life and her journey toward shaping the future of computing:

1. 1815: Birth

    Augusta Ada Byron is born on December 10 in London, England, to the poet Lord Byron and Lady Annabella Milbanke Byron.

2. 1816: Parents Separate

    Lord Byron leaves England; Ada is raised by her mother, who emphasizes mathematics to counterbalance her father's "poetic" influence.

3. 1833: Meeting Charles Babbage

    At age 17, Ada encounters Babbage's Difference Engine prototype at a social gathering, sparking a lifelong fascination with mechanical computation.

4. 1835: Marriage
   Ada marries William King, who later becomes the Earl of Lovelace, making her the Countess of Lovelace.

5. 1842–1843: Translating Menabrea's Paper
   Ada translates Luigi Menabrea's work on Babbage's Analytical Engine and adds extensive notes, which include the first "computer program."

6. 1843: Publication of Ada's Notes
   Her annotated translation is published, introducing the idea that machines could handle symbols and be "programmed."

7. 1852: Passing

    Ada Lovelace dies on November 27 at age 36,
    from complications believed to be uterine cancer.

8. 1970s: Re-Emergence of Ada's Work

    Historians rediscover her notes, hailing her as the
    first computer programmer. The U.S.
    Department of Defense names a programming
    language "Ada."

9. Today: Lasting Influence

    Celebrated for her visionary ideas on computing,
    Ada Lovelace remains a symbol of creativity,
    perseverance, and the power of interdisciplinary
    thinking.

CHAPTER 9: QUICK-FACT SIDEBARS

1. [Fun Fact #1: The "Princess of Parallelograms"]

   Ada's mother, Lady Byron, earned the nickname "Princess of Parallelograms" for her love of geometry. She made sure Ada studied math intensely from a young age to avoid the "poetic madness" she saw in Lord Byron.

2. [Fun Fact #2: A Poet's Legacy]

   Lord Byron is best known for his works like *Don Juan* and *Childe Harold's Pilgrimage*. Despite Ada's strong math leanings, she inherited some of her father's imaginative flair, blending creativity with logic.

3. [Fun Fact #3: Notes Longer Than the Original!]

Ada's Notes on Menabrea's paper were so extensive that they ended up being about three times longer than the paper itself, showcasing her deep insight into Babbage's Engine.

4. [Fun Fact #4: Flying Ambitions]

As a child, Ada tried to design a flying machine. She studied bird wings and called herself "Lady Fairy," indicating she had a vivid imagination even when focused on mechanical details.

5. [In Her Time: Victorian Constraints]

Women of Ada's status weren't encouraged to pursue mathematics or science. Many assumed "rational thinking" was a man's domain. Ada's achievements are all the more extraordinary given these social hurdles.

CHAPTER 10: LOOKING BACK, LOOKING FORWARD

A da Lovelace is often called the "Enchantress of Numbers," an apt description for someone who saw magical possibilities in a web of gears, cogs, and algorithms. She believed that with the right instructions, a machine could go beyond arithmetic to transform information, be it letters, notes, or even music.

Her greatest legacy is the concept of programmability — the idea that by breaking a task into logical steps and carefully encoding those steps, we can make a machine carry out complex processes on our behalf. This vision laid the groundwork for modern computers, even though actual electronic computers wouldn't appear until almost a hundred years after her death.

When we use smartphones, tablets, or personal computers, we're effectively living in the future Ada predicted. Our devices process enormous amounts of data in seconds, "understanding" images, text, and sounds in the form of binary numbers. That's the direct line from Ada Lovelace's 19th-century Notes to the 21st-century technology that surrounds us.

But Ada's story is also about challenging societal norms. She was a high-society woman in Victorian England, yet she stepped outside the narrow expectations placed on her gender to pursue mathematics at a high level. She collaborated with scientists, published academic work, and questioned whether a machine could ever think like a human. In doing so, she opened doors—for herself and for future generations of women in science and technology.

Where might Ada's ideas lead next? Today, scientists and innovators explore machine learning, artificial intelligence, quantum computing, and more. We're wrestling with questions about whether computers can ever truly be creative, or if they're limited to the algorithms humans design. These are the same fundamental issues Ada raised nearly two centuries ago.

As you reflect on her journey, let Ada's curiosity and determination inspire you to see the bigger picture—to look at a problem and ask, "What if?" Like Ada, don't be afraid to merge imagination with logic, or to dive into fields that others might overlook or underestimate. The next big leap in technology might come from someone who dares to dream as Ada did, uniting seemingly opposite forces—math and art, logic and creativity—to spark a new revolution.

GLOSSARY

- Algorithm: A set of step-by-step instructions for solving a problem or completing a task. In computing, algorithms are the foundation of all programming.

- Analytical Engine: Charles Babbage's proposed mechanical computer, designed to be programmable using punch cards. It was never fully built, but Ada Lovelace's notes on it are considered the first computer programs.

- Bernoulli Numbers: A sequence of numbers with special properties in mathematics, used in complex calculations. Ada wrote instructions on how the Analytical Engine could compute these numbers.

- Difference Engine: Babbage's earlier invention, intended to automate arithmetic calculations (like polynomial functions). It's less advanced than the Analytical Engine but paved the way for mechanical computing.

- General-Purpose Computing: The idea that a single machine can be programmed to perform a variety of tasks, rather than just one specialized function. Ada saw this as the future of Babbage's engine.

- High Society: The social elite of Victorian England, which had strict expectations about behavior, etiquette, and roles—especially for women.

- Punch Cards: Stiff paper cards with holes punched in specific patterns to encode data or instructions. Early computers, and even some voting systems, used these to input commands.

- Uterine Cancer: A type of cancer affecting the uterus. Though medicine in Ada's time was basic, historians believe this was the illness that led to her early death.

Author's Note / Next Steps

Thank you for diving into the fascinating world of Ada Lovelace with me! Writing this book reminded me how easy it can be to overlook pioneers—especially women—whose groundbreaking ideas remain hidden for decades or even centuries. Ada's story shows that sheer determination and imagination can triumph over societal limits, whether that means learning math in an era that discouraged women from studying it, or envisioning computers long before technology caught up.

If Ada Lovelace's story has inspired you to delve deeper into mathematics and computing, consider exploring:

1. Coding Basics: Learn a programming language like Scratch or Python. By creating your own simple programs, you'll see firsthand how

algorithms bring computers to life—just like Ada imagined.

2. History of Computing: Read about other inventors like Charles Babbage or Alan Turing, or watch online videos about the evolution of computers from mechanical devices to modern electronics.

3. STE(A)M Activities: Combining Art with STEM (Science, Technology, Engineering, Math) can unlock creative solutions. Maybe design your own "machine" out of cardboard and craft materials or compose a simple melody in code.

Most of all, remember that Ada Lovelace believed anyone with passion and curiosity could push the boundaries of what's possible. Her story resonates across time, proving that innovation can bloom under even the strictest constraints. Whether your interests lean toward music, art, math, or building robots, the real magic happens when you let these subjects overlap in surprising ways.

So, keep asking big questions, keep tinkering with new ideas, and don't let obstacles hold you back. Ada never did. Who knows—maybe you'll be the next visionary who dares to see beyond the present into a future the rest of the world has yet to imagine!

Made in the USA
Monee, IL
27 March 2025

14733184R00039